PAR⊕USIA
Parousia Christian Poetry Chapbook

VOTE FOR

JESUS

Olatokun Oluwafemi

Vote For Jesus

Olatokun Oluwafemi

PAROUSIA

Parousia Christian Poetry Chapbook No 9 ~ 2020 Series

Vote for Jesus by Femi Olatokun
Copyright © Olatokun Oluwafemi 2020

Published in Nigeria by
Parousia
(Parousia Reads and Magazine)

Address: 138, Ext II, by DLBC Pipeline, Kubwa, Abuja, FCT, Nigeria.
Correspondence Address: 1, OSS Ltd, Rufai Olayiwola Complex, Benjamin Bus Stop, Eleyele, Ibadan, Oyo State, Nigeria.

Phone No: +2347030874764, +2348128406752,
Email: publishing@parousiareads.com
Website: www.parousiareads.com

Cover Concept and Design: www.dabrandcity.com
Book Design: Tola Ijalusi

Parousia welcomes the submission of literary works for free publication
Email: submissions@parousiamagazine.com
Website: www.parousiamagazine.com

PAR⊕USIA

Contents

Acknowledgements

God's love for me has always been the true source of my motivation and encouragement. May His praise forever dwell in my heart and on my lips and may the light of His salvation always encompass me in the course of my journey on earth. This work is dedicated to Him who is the greatest lover and the only true forgiver of sins who loves all sinners but not their sins.

My sincere appreciation goes to my parents, Mr. Albert and Funmilayo Olatokun, all my siblings, and all the members of my family as well. Your love is my unending song in the course of my wonderful journey. I am extremely grateful to Olufemi Samson, Marcus Victor, Mrs. Clara Irabor, Marcel Ojo, Famadeji Emmanuel, Mrs. Lilian Afenkhide, Mrs. Olajumoke Aroso Olusola, Mrs. Favour Oyakhire, Fatayo Sunday, Prince Chimaobi, Mr. Awoyale, and Ayeyemi Olabisi for their love and understanding. I am also greatly indebted to Mr. Akinfoyewa Adeniyi, Azuoma Sophie, Mr. Olatunbosun Taofeek, and many others too numerous to be mentioned for the positive review. May you all be richly rewarded by God in Jesus' name.

All the Biblical quotations in this collection are taken from the King James Version of the Holy Bible. The quote, "Come hither!" Line 81 of *The Two Witness* is also taken from Rev 11:12(KJV) and also "Before Abraham was, I am" Line 11 and 12 is taken from John 8:58(KJV). I remain grateful to KJV for these.

Lastly, it is my belief and prayer that whosoever reads this work will be tremendously blessed and will forever have God as his or her companion. Thanks and God bless. Shalom.

Olatokun Oluwafemi A

Foreword

Poetry still remains the best means of communication between God and man. It is the language used when men speak like kings, heroes of faith or angels, since it is capable of transporting meaning, emotion, and beauty all harmoniously wrapped together into one meaningful whole at the same time. It gives wings to souls and strengthens their limbs to rise above the storms of life and establishes a nexus with the throne of the Father of all mankind. The heights attained by poetry remains matchless till date and great poets in the past have also explored it to further strengthen the faith of men and likewise, it is still of great value in this contemporary period. It is noteworthy that many of our great hymns are direct products of poetry. In fact, immense benefits can be derived from it. Be that as it may, the legacy poets of this age will leave behind should be of great concern to all Christian poets.

I will not mince my words. The perilous time is here! Love is becoming cold among human beings, piety is frowned upon in human society, and humility is seen in the light of stupidity. In short, many are turning their backs on every form of Godliness. In a time like this, we dare not fold our hands and watch. We must write and we can write to arouse the consciousness of men to strengthen the weak, heal the sick, and uphold the faith of Christians living in this unusual time. Simply put, Christians have a lot to do. We have to love more, give more and share more. Let there be unity and a common goal and let us learn to provide succor to the disheartened and the wounded soldiers in our midst. They must never be abandoned in the face of challenges. The battle is tough and it may not be easy for others to love God the way we do, but we can enlighten them and show them the way by voting for Jesus in all we do.

Vote for Jesus is both a call and a response in a world where the Church of God has to firmly stand on its feet and make great exploits in order not to lose its sheep to the wolves of this world. As a call, *Vote for Jesus* delineates the differences between human promises and divine promises; thereby, exposing the frailties of all men. The human soul hankers for satisfaction but this can only be achieved if we vote to be part of the glorious kingdom. But while waiting for the kingdom, let us explore the radiance of God that transcends excellence in elegance by honoring, praising, and loving Him with all our hearts. So as you read, open your mind and let the verses unite your soul with the elegance of our creator.

Vote for Jesus also explores many Christian themes. Some of them are self-will, obedience, gratitude, prayer, haughtiness, and deafness. Four sonnets are dedicated to deafness as a theme since it has been discovered that human beings are always eager to talk to God in prayers but only a few are actually ready to listen and obey His voice. This is terrible and disheartening! Also, as a warning in a time like this, in *The Two Witnesses*, a parallel is drawn between what happened before Sodom and Gomorrah were consumed by the wrath of God. This is not to scare anybody but to draw our attention to two things. One, the similarity between the vices common in those cities and those sprouting in our midst today. Two, the identity of the two witnesses who according to the Book of Revelation will visit the earth towards the end of time just like the way they went to the cities of Sodom and Gomorrah after leaving Abraham in Mamre. These are well documented in the

Holy Bible. Read Revelation 11: 3- 12, Zechariah 4: 14, Genesis 18:2, and Genesis 19: 1 for more on this. Since we all know that this world will no doubt fade away, let us hold unto Christ "who is holy, harmless, undefiled, separate from sinners, and made higher than the heavens" [a] as the mediator of the new testament" and whose reign alone is capable of wiping all our tears and supplying our needs because He has said it that only those "that overcometh shall inherit all things; and I will be his God, and he shall be my son"[b]. So in order to overcome, vote for Jesus because a vote for Jesus is a win for you.

Shalom,

Olatokun Oluwafemi A

July 2020.

[a] Hebrew 7:26

[b] Revelation 21:7

Blurb

These soul-lifting poems are truly enthralling in a powerful manner. The simplicity and authenticity of the diction and messages are highly remarkable. A suitable companion in the lives of contemporary Christians.

Akinfoyewa Adeniyi, Lecturer, Author, and Publisher.

Hallowed Homage (one of the poems in Vote for Jesus) shows gratitude and exaltation. The poet shows with his artistry the depth of faith he has in his Maker, placing him supreme with a surreal feeling as the words flow so tender yet very strong with his exaltation.

Azuoma Sophie, Poet.

VOTE FOR JESUS

Is there enough water to quench human thirst?
Are there enough rains to please the desert's tongue?
Are two hands enough to feed the human mouth?
Is one tongue enough to satisfy the human soul?
Oh! Many have traveled back and forth in life
Searching for satisfaction but still left unsatisfied
And many have cried out their hearts while waiting
For mirages to yield water to quench their thirst
But for how long will the waiters be made to wait?

The waiting seems to be over
As posters and adverts announce the arrival of election
And at least with a new government,
Hope seems to be on the horizon for the human soul.

Election year usually comes with promises
And slogans from the organs of political parties
Entice human souls and enslave their thumbprints
And silly sentiments join to drive home
Sweet stories that are better left unheard
Into the human ears that never get tired
Of listening and listening and listening
To old tales told in new ways by sweetened tongues
As the drums in the human ears
Can never be filled to its brim.

At once, sweet dreams drift unhindered
Due to the expectation of satisfaction
In the lives of the hopefuls
Who usually look forward and dream of a better world.
Alas! Election year usually comes and leaves
And regimes are changed from time to time.

Yet, promises made are left unfulfilled
And so the human souls become sad
Due to the burden of broken promises.
" Oh! They are not good for anything!"
Those with great courage will shout
With the conclusion that those in power
Can never be trusted in any wise:
For how long will time waste while waiters wait?

" Will they ever keep their promises?"
This question baffles you without a doubt
But have you ever asked yourself this:
"Are they in a position to keep promises?"
Human promises are mostly made to be broken;
Only divine promises are certain once spoken.

While some go too far towards the left,
Leaving too much to be desired;
Others go too far towards the right
Leaving too little to keep people satisfied.
Only Jesus fills all squares and round holes
Without leaving just a space in error
For only He is capable of keeping promises.
So don't be angry when they disappoint
As that may be too harsh on them
For no human being possesses enough skills
To direct a government that will benefit all
And neither you, they nor I can boast of such
Because even when those in power mean the best
What about those they surround themselves with?
When the clouds fail to help at night,
Even Sirius and Arcturus do hide in the holes of the sky!

If with the mere print of your finger,
You are capable of changing the government.
There is a decision you can take today
That will put you in government eternally
And fill your heart with joy that knows no end
And that is by voting for Jesus.
Listen: while a vote for others is a win for them,
A vote for Jesus is a win for you.

You have voted times without number and lost
And even when those you voted for won,
You still lost as many of your yearnings were left unsatisfied:
Aren't these telltale signs that human wants are insatiable?
Why can't you reconsider your way today?
Reflect, rethink, and decide without delay.
Some in government simply have their best.
They lick wealth like honey but still wail afterwards,
But how sweeter will the Kingdom of Christ be!

No human government possesses the skills
To make all happy at the same time
And even those who they make happy
Still have one or two things that are left untouched.
So it is only with the arrival of Christ
And the inception of His millennial reign
That you, all and I can actually enjoy in full
For the bliss obtained in Jesus is pure and eternal.
So let us make haste and vote for Him today
For a vote for Jesus is a vote for eternal life
And only He can satisfy the desire of all nations.
So vote for Jesus and vote for eternal bliss;
Vote for Jesus and gain eternal happiness.

HALLOWED HOMAGE

Hallowed homage to Lord God Almighty,
The owner and ruler of the universe,
Before whom the twenty-four elders
Cast their crowns in adoration and worship
While the four living creatures rest not
In their changeless chants of Holy! Holy!! Holy!!!
To display their extreme sense of gratitude.
Your majesty, Lord God, is indescribable!
Your majesty, Elohim, is unassailable!
And your majesty, Jehovah, is unfathomable!

Hallowed homage, Eternal Father of all mankind.
Who will not bow before you
When even the Seraphim find your face
Too holy to behold and Cherubim render fiery services
While powerful angels tremble before your throne.
Your dominion, Lord God, will eternally remain impeccable!
Your dominion, our God, will eternally remain immutable!
Your dominion, my God, will eternally remain
unquestionable!

Hallowed homage, Power that exceeds power
And exudes power and consumes power!
No word can depict the gracefulness of your glory.
Or, how shall I describe You
When just your radiance transcends excellence in elegance?
How shall I praise You
When only the girdle of your praise
Is broader than the broadest garment
Of all human languages?
I AM THAT I AM, only You are worthy to be praised
For the destiny of the world rests solely
In your tireless palms.

THE TWO WITNESSES

Christ will come and will not delay.
His coming is for an appointed time.
He who came with love and salvation
Will return with justice and judgment
To judge the inhabitants of the earth
And rightly reward the righteous.

His going forth has been of old
For from Him, who preceded the beginning,
Proceeded the beginning
And little did many know when He proclaimed:
"Before Abraham was, I AM."

"Before Abraham was, I AM",
Proclaimed He from whom Father Abraham
 Gained His very existence
And yet many doubted the claim
When even Abraham was glad to set his eyes
On the Ever-living Word of Life.
Unknown to them, God didn't hide
From Abraham that thing which He will do.

Right here on earth, He visited Abraham in Mamre
Who saw in Him the God of all the earth
Just like Photini the Samaritan woman at Sychar
Found Him and called Him the Saviour of the world.

Are you still in the flesh like Old Thomas?
Cast the shadow of your doubts away
And for once embrace the light of the truth
For it is only in it exceeding joy can be found.

Who visited Abraham in Mamre let us ask?
And can God the Almighty be seen with the human eyes?
I know HIS voice may at times be heard
When HE alone wants it so,
But He can only be seen through the figure of
His only begotten Son:
He who has seen Christ has seen God.

Three men visited Abraham in Mamre
But only two went to Sodom while Abraham
Stood before the third, "the Lord of all the earth"
Who he called: "The Judge of all the earth."

Who are these two that went along with the Lord
To accomplish His divine purposes?
Are these not the two olive trees
Who were mightily revealed to Zechariah
And later confirmed by John?

Mrs. Zebedee wanted better things.
The heaven must have been opened for her
And she must have seen powerful visions
That drove her to demand from Jesus
That her children should be allowed to take
The positions of the two witnesses
Which unknown to her, can only be chosen by God.
Clever she was indeed!
Divine she was, no doubt!
Who among the mortals can reject
The lure of fame and power
And the opportunity of occupying enviable positions
And most importantly, when closeness
To the Son of the Most High is involved?

These two are the closest to the Son of Man
And shall crown the seal of evangelism
Before the second coming of my master.
Were they not the last witnesses
 Against unrepentant Sodom and Gomorrah
Before the wrath of God took the path of justice
And shall they not be here once again
To witness against not a part but the whole world
Before the final trumpet?

These anointed ones are Mighty beings
For they shall drink from the cup that Jesus drank
And be baptized still with His baptism.
Power shall be given to them by God
To witness for a thousand two hundred and sixty days
And shall they not with holy power once again
Deal with those who oppose the gospel truth
Just like blindness was unleashed
On the immoral inhabitants of Sodom and Gomorrah?

O Christians, this is another sign to watch for.
Although they shall be martyred
This is just to fulfil prophecy
And make them fully worthy of glory at last
And even as Christ rose and ascended into heaven,
So shall these be resurrected with "come hither!"
To cast shame and fear on those who opposed the Word
And this shall be later crowned with judgement
Heavier than any ever witnessed before on earth.

Christ of God will come! The son of God will come!
He will appear at the appointed hour
No delay! No lateness! No change of mind

For He is the God of all the earth
And His two witnesses are the two olive trees;
They are the two candlesticks
Which usually accompany His journey
Just like when He sent the disciples in twos
And when Elijah and Moses visited Him on the mountain.
Christians, only a little of this is known to men
But God at the end will fully reveal it
To those who stay awake at their post:
Christ will come and will not delay.
His coming is for an appointed time!

Dedicated to my Dad who exposed me to the word of God from a tender age.

SELF-WILLED

"My child, do not go!"
Said He. "Stay beside me and grow."
"Abba Father, please let me try." Replied I
As my heart raced rapidly in a bid
To join the human race.
"The roads are rough and the nights are dark
And each day dawns with a divisive spark
And over there are friendly enemies
And friends that are still friends to your enemies."
All these He added with a loving tone:
"The battles are endless; winning in one context
Is a ticket for participation in the next!"
I shrugged, grew sadder
And concluded that He desired to deny me
The joy of venturing.

He looked me in the eyes.
O! How great His love is!
He drew me close
And I burst into tears
But still, the fire burns deep down within me
And I let out a cry:
"Abba Father, please grant my wish.
You know everything.
You know how much I love You.
I just want to have a first-hand experience.
Just let Your love keep burning in me."
Not even Peter the Rock could have said it better!

I knew I was self-willed
And He declared:
"I will. But know that over there,

You dare not even trust the air
Since there is evil and there is goodness;
There is light and there is darkness.
Negative forces are in constant struggle,
They shift from one angle to another angle,
To subdue the domination of positive forces
And so with great anger, they usually raise their voices.
Their fields are gardens of flawless beauty
Where love loves to perform its duty;
Their fields are battlegrounds of bloody wars
Fought with high hatred, resulting in fatal sores.
And worst of all,
Still lingering after their downfall
Is the putrid smell of sins and crimes
Which like clouds cover millions of miles"
He paused and then added:
"But I will never leave you alone."
With these reassuring words, I closed my eyes
To travel through the stars.

My wish was granted
And I conquered millions of miles
Within minutes, and
I arrived.
I looked up but His Face
Was so far away
And I cried and cried and cried
And as I let out my vagitus,
I discovered I was surrounded by blood
And a woman in great pain smiled at me
But her smile cannot be compared to what
I used to know up there.

As always is,

His words have proved to be true
And I have proceeded
From one battle to another
Because I must cap a victory
With another victory, so
Forgiveness for my sins I plead
And now, how I wish I was not self-willed
And I wish the more now
(Though it is worth venturing)
To be obedient to His will not mine
For He knows the best for me.

BACK TO THE RIGHT PATH

Great then was their joy in Eden
Where everything worked well with love
For God worked with them every day,
Perfecting the beauty of men.
Mercy descended from above
To supply their needs every day:
How good will it be to go back!

Tragic was the day things went wrong.
Lucifer looted seeds of life;
Satan sat and spoiled everything.
Since then we have lost our good song.
All we have now is sordid strife
And to labour for everything:
Won't it be good to just go back?

Men turned vultures, striving to feed
For everything has been reversed
And Love walked no more among them!
Many are now monsters of greed;
More and more, condition worsened
And pure love is now a rare gem:
Won't it be good if we turn back?

The old role we played with the rule,
Is our new ropes of hope to cope
And what we suffered in the past,
We are still facing like a fool.
We grope for the way but no hope
For this our short life cannot last
Till to the Maker we go back!

The pure truth is that we are lost
And there is one way of solving this;
That's going back to the Maker
For on the cross, Christ paid the cost
To bring us back the Eden's bliss.
Our ways let us reconsider:
It will be good if we go back.

Stop aggravating these problems
Like flies caught in the spider web,
Trying to play wise with the rule!
Let's accept the rules as emblems
Then all our problems will all ebb
And hot conditions will turn cool
If to God we try to turn back.

GIVING THANKS

Oh! How good it is to give thanks
To the Ever-merciful God
And this costs nothing to perform
And those who offer gratitude
Are sure to receive many more.

No matter how harsh the hardship,
There are still many good reasons
To continue in giving thanks.
That was what three wise men set out to prove,
Each offering thanks based on his state.

"Good Lord, I give thanks", said the first
"For this rich meal", he continued:
"Was not supplied by my wisdom or power
But I got it through your grace alone.
Lord, accept the thanks of your grateful son".

The audience readily reasoned among themselves
That he had very good reasons to offer thanks:
"Who will not be glad for such a rich meal?" They asked.
After this, they waited anxiously
For what the next man who was served gruel would say.

"God, I am so grateful. Accept my thanks", said he
"For supplying this unexpected meal.
It may be little, but I'm sure some had none.
Still, you granted me the grace to consume it.
Lord, accept the thanks of your faithful son".

The audience were not much surprised
But started laughing at the third who had none.

He was a tall old man with deep set eyes.
They concluded he would not even make it
To the podium. But slowly he made his way and arrived!

"Good Lord, accept my thanks", said the man.
Though I had nothing to feed on
But some ate and died in the process through poison
And here today against expectation I'm still alive.
Lord, accept the thanks of your hopeful son".

On hearing this, the audience were confounded
And they too started thanking the Almighty,
Counting their blessings one by one
And felt sorry for their past ungratefulness.
Even on their way home, songs of praises they sang.

So brethren, in any condition in life,
It is a must to render praises to God
For all the good things He has done and will do
And for all the evils He has saved us from
For thanksgiving comes only from a wise heart.

ON MY KNEES

Now, my thoughts overflow
And in their races run
In criss-cross lines across my heart.
Some swell to bring tears to my eyes
As sharp onions do
And some force my heart to beat faster,
Faster till I am in a rage.

Burdened by loads
Too heavy for porters as mortals to bear,
Strength betrayed my trust.
Weary legs bow to relentless distance
Even as my trust in strength
Failed to take me far.
Gone is my strength
As frail limbs have failed to keep them in
And I am indeed left here alone at last.

This is hard to puzzle out
For wisdom fails to show me
How to add an
Inch to my height!

My trust in wisdom
Only helps a little here
As not even wisdom but ropes
Are the only conjunctions
That can bind woods together
And even as days keep turning into nights before fading,
My wisdom failed to tell them
Halt!
And so, gnats in their multitudes swarm on my frailties.

Now, resting on the words of Christ alone,
My faith bends my knees
And as I am on my bended knees,
My fears begin to fade.
My fears begin to fade
As those mountains like ships begin to sail away.

DO NOT LISTEN TO ME

Do not listen to me, O Lord
And kindly disregard my prayers even if I kneel
To implore you to grant me
The pride of the heart.
Even if every nation pleads on my behalf,
Kindly turn your loving face away!
O Lord, no matter how sweet my voice is;
No matter how pleasant I sound;
Dear Lord, do not listen to me.

Dear loving Lord, grant me all. I mean all
But take haughtiness far from me:
Deprive me of it!
Deaden my senses to it!
Divert my anger towards it
And set Swords of Flame between me and it!
Grant me the grace to see myself as I am:
Nothing! A common clay, a dwindling dust
And an actual ash!

When I lower my gaze,
Let it be to lift others up;
Do not let me turn left or right,
If not to save those who are astray;
And when my hands I raise towards the sky,
It should never be to rain slaps on the weak
But to render due praises
To your holy name
And then Lord, you can now listen
To the sweet sounds of my sweetest praise.

SIN AND DEATH

It was one hot afternoon,
Men from all corners gathered
To watch what would happen soon
Where two friends were to be judged,
Charged with a hot mass murder case.
The evidence was so clear
And so the people gave thanks
To the police who were there
For a job well done under the moon.

People clustered around the scene
As the two friends were brought down
Just to know the worse between
Them: no mercy to be shown
To neither of the two bad friends.
Just men swore that afternoon
To put an end to such trends.
They must be judged that same noon
For the people who came were so keen.

The first one looked so friendly
His name was revealed as Sin.
The other looked so ugly,
Named Death, and he was so thin.
Each claimed innocence but lacked proof;
Watched with mock solemnity
Just to hide their cloven hoof
And escaped the penalty
Meant to eviscerate their belly.

Finally, they kissed the dust

Each with his mouth confessing.
They were judged as the Judge must:
Each was to die by hanging!
So to any doubting Thomas,
'Twas sin that invited death!
So of the two, Sin is worse
Unknown to many on earth:
No Sin, no Death! Flee from sin: adjust!

O HOLY SPIRIT!

I am standing against forces bent on bending me!
I am quenching fire revolving to envelope and engulf me!
I am holding on, tightly, with all my sinew
And in desperation to live, death I defy,
Calling my strength to order,
Drawing the powers in my inner eyes
To ward off pure darkness, thick as a wall.
I can never be afraid
As I'm standing where there exists no fear!

Though feeble strength I possess;
The poor frailties of all flesh,
Against their desires, their evil wishes,
I will stand like the pillars of heaven;
I will stand to regain and repossess.

O Holy Spirit,
You, I cannot see; You are invisible!
I am stretching now beyond human limits.
I am here but You are everywhere.
O hold me, Holy Spirit!
O fill me, Creator Spirit!

Open my eyes
Let me gently rise
In faith and in victory.
Hold me and when the battle is over,
Let me safely land on the glorious land
For enough for me is your Hand,
O Holy Spirit of the Ever-living God.

SONNET – DEAFNESS

I

Our love of God in endless confessions.
In His presence, pure obedience in praise.
Always ready, our needs and pains to raise
And partly tell one of our transgressions.
Our desire for success and progressions;
Our call for fire and thunder to raze
For seeds of evil must die in the blaze
And men in peace must gain their possessions.
O slowly our prayers move through the air
And it seems our minds only pray in vain
For all seems to be lost in the process
But all, the Invisible proves to hear
"Listen! " In love, He answers for our pain:
" All have dulled their ears to proper deafness."

II

" Like lost dogs, my clarion calls they ignore,
Exerting the muscles of their small lips,
They growl and bark like an orphan that weeps.
Still at nights, have wounds that pain to the core.
As keys of greed lead to an empty door
They pray in volumes but only one creeps
Like crowded grains or seeds in worn-out heaps
Where one out of many grows for the store.
They hanker after different kinds of stuff
For their own good, these I have rejected.
They must complain for they will not listen
Smooth words hindered for their hearts are so rough
And the answered goes unappreciated
The best to do is call them to reason.

III

Back to the world of words O wandering lobes,
Unfold your wild wings till the winds obey.
Revolve in circles and trap words this way.
Train the lips of the ear to move like robes
Till the unspoken yield to constant probes
And the current of thoughts distill and stay
For the ears to unravel as we pray
In constancy, not on and off like strobes.
Then will this lonely earth be lifted up
And the distance in the vast sphere will flee
For heaven to embrace the earth with cheers;
Men shall smile and lamentations shall stop
As endless treasures shall flow like the sea
And praises shall replace prayers and tears.

IV

Why cry, when your maker has endowed you
With the drippings of honey for your taste
And the smooth sweet tomato for your paste
And still, you lack not the cool morning dew
And the sweet birds fail not to pay their due.
Why will you continue to run and haste
In your anger, these sweet things suffer waste
As they rot with old age, though born as new.
Why watch in helpless vain, things in your care
And in morbid dread burn the cords of life?
Only an arrogant sword spoils its ward.
Search, search! These wonders around you are rare,
Ages can never pay their price in half.
So, tune in to be in tune with your Lord.

GOD NEVER SLEEPS

Days are crowned by tomorrows
Followed by vivid blessings,
Witnesses to His unfailing grace.

And, if we live
To witness tomorrows,
For from death's grip daily we return;
This is only through His mercies obtained.
If happiness we lick with joy and frown at sorrows;
Praises, we ought to give.

To live a day more
Is simple but simply beyond our reach
But all, after vanities run
When all good things abound in His store.

Good things every second we lick;
The air we breathe, the world we live in.
Think about the zillions they run to
Years after years.
Can we repay a fraction of it?

We cannot pay a fraction of it
But still at nights,
We lower our praises and our heads:
Helpless on our different beds
But He remains faithful, waking us up
The following day
Because when we sleep as the others sleep,
Quenching all evils that creep
Is Jehovah, who will never sleep.

Biography:

OLATOKUN OLUWAFEMI A, a poet, playwright, novelist, short-story writer, song writer and social crusader, is a diligent man of many talents. He lives in Lagos, Nigeria. He graduated from the National Open University of Nigeria in 2015 with an honours degree in English Language.

He is a realist and a conscientious being who spills the oil of words on pages like correction fluid with the aim of correcting social and spiritual ills in human society and also endows words with wings to fly the message of reorientation, rejuvenation, and hope to every beautiful creation of God. He is an ardent lover of Christ and he strongly believes that the gospel must be preached by every possible means.

He is the author of *The Fundamentals of Oral English* for *All Students, It is my Right* (A Play), *Reorientation* (Poetry) and many other academic and literary works. He is a highly seasoned English teacher and currently teaches at Livingstone College, Lagos.

PAROUSIA READS

Parousia Reads is a publishing firm that will make your dreams come true. Our diverse offers of services including our bookstore exist solely for this purpose.

At Parousia Reads, we're dedicated to helping authors build their writing careers. From editorial and production to promotion, distribution, and sales, our focus is on working with our authors to reach our readers. We are committed to providing the highest level of sales and distribution service to authors. With us, be rest assured that the book you are publishing or buying from our bookstore is the best it could be.

We are ready to help you achieve your dream.

You can also send us a mail at

publishing@parousiareads.com

To check out our services, visit

www.parousiareads.com